Garfield

"I HATE MONDAY"

BY: JIM DAVIS

Ravette London

This edition first published by
Ravette Limited 1986

───────────────────────────

Printed and bound in Great Britain
for Ravette Limited,
12 Star Road, Partridge Green,
Horsham, Sussex RH13 8RA
by William Clowes Limited, Beccles and London.

ISBN 0 948456 17 5

"I HATE MONDAY"

As you can see, Garfield's pet hate is MONDAY and the alarming regularity with which it arrives and although Garfield is renowned for his appetite, he's no "Glutton for Punishment".

WELL, I WONDER WHAT'S GOING TO HAPPEN TO ME TODAY

JIM DAVIS   12-27

BLAT!

© 1982 United Feature Syndicate, Inc.

MONDAY MOVES IN A MYSTERIOUS WAY

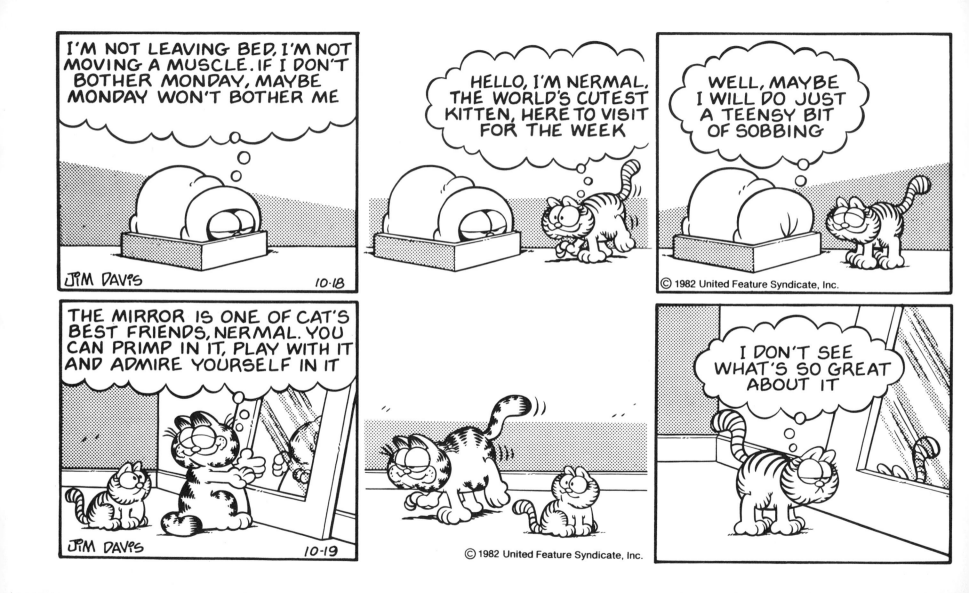

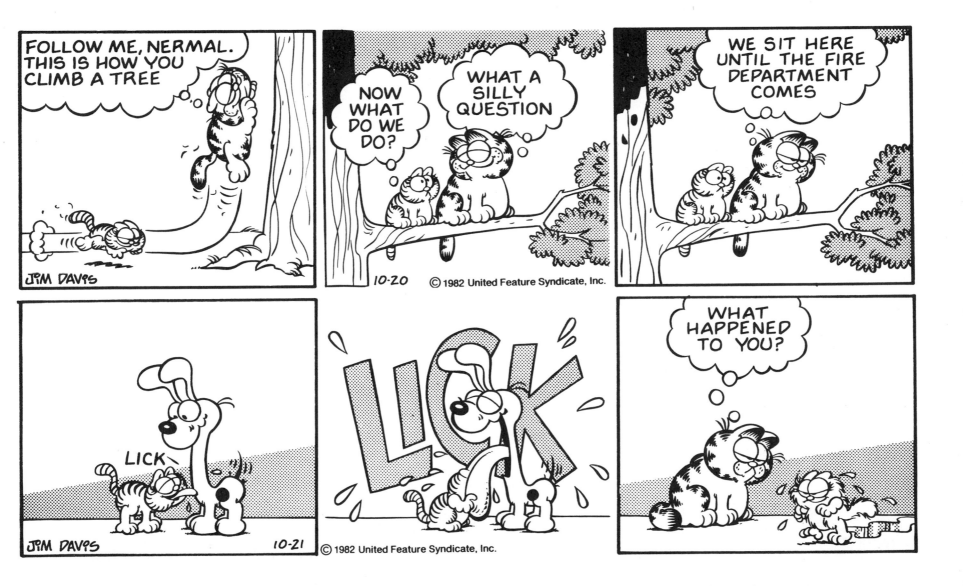

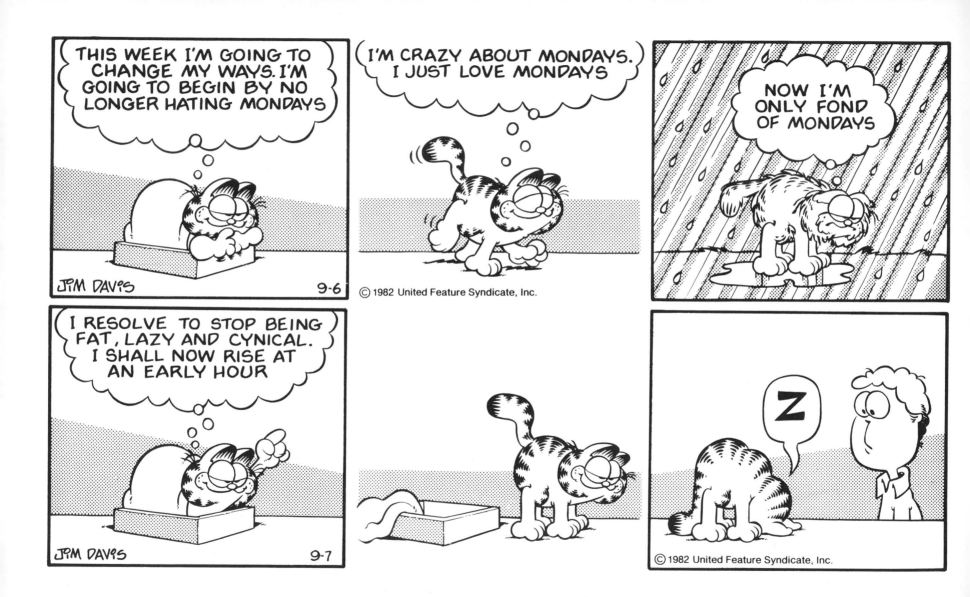

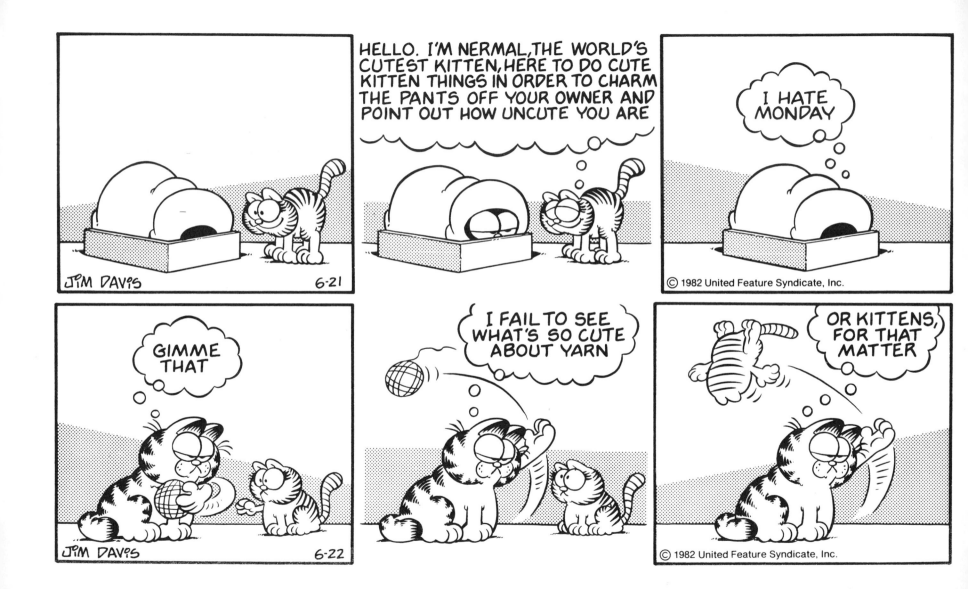